What happens when I die?

And other questions about heaven, hell and the life to come

Marcus Nodder

Questions
Christians ask

What happens when I die?
And other questions about heaven, hell and the life to come
Part of the *Questions Christians Ask* series
© Marcus Nodder/The Good Book Company, 2013.
Reprinted 2013, 2018 with additions.

Published by
The Good Book Company
Tel (UK): 0333 123 0880;
Tel (North America): (1) 866 244 2165
International: +44 (0) 208 942 0880
Email (UK): info@thegoodbook.co.uk
Email (North America): info@thegoodbook.com

Websites
UK & Europe: www.thegoodbook.co.uk
North America: www.thegoodbook.com
Australia: www.thegoodbook.com.au
New Zealand: www.thegoodbook.co.nz

ISBN: 9781908762337 | Printed in the UK

Design by André Parker

Contents

In memory of Mum and Dad,
now with the Lord

Introduction

It was a Saturday morning when we got the phone-call from my mother. It was hard to make out everything she said given that she was so distressed, but it was something to do with my father having collapsed.

He was only 62 and had no health problems we were aware of, so the news that he was unwell came very much out of the blue. Ten minutes later the phone rang again. This time it was a good family friend who was there with mum. She was sorry to have to tell me that my father was dead.

One minute he'd been working away at his desk in his study at home (he was a church minister); the next he was lying on the floor dead. Apparently he would have known very little about it. Undiagnosed heart problem. It would have been as sudden as flicking a switch and turning off a light.

That was 12 years ago. My mother still finds Saturdays hard and has never really got used to living on her own. His retirement was only a few years away and they had started making plans and were looking forward to having more time together and with the family. I look at our four kids growing up and can't help but feel a sadness that they never knew their grandfather. He was so great with kids and they would have loved him so much. And personally, I just miss him—very much.

* * *

Few experiences in life are as painful as the loss of a loved one. Only those who have been through bereavement themselves can really understand what it is like.

If that is your situation, you may have picked up this book looking for hope and comfort and answers.

We will certainly get to answers. But in looking at the subject of death from the Bible, we will also be forced to face up to some uncomfortable truths, one of which is the reality of our own death. If you've just been diagnosed with a terminal illness, you will need no convincing of this, but for the rest of us Sigmund Freud was onto something when he once wrote: "No-one really believes in his own death".

For most of us death is something that happens to other people. We read about it in the papers, we see it on TV or even experience it in our wider families, but we don't think it's going to happen to us. But it will. And we need to prepare for it. Have you come to terms with the inconvenient truth of your own death?

Some cope with the prospect of death by joking and making light of it. Others use language which hides the awful reality of death. They speak of someone as having "passed on", "passed away" or being "no longer with us". Some cling to vague hopes that everything will turn out alright and that everyone goes to a better place, while others proclaim with confidence that death is the absolute end. But in neither case is this belief anything more than wishful thinking.

Yet others simply refuse to talk about death. It's as if there's a conspiracy of silence. People are dying in our communities every day and yet you'd hardly know. The dead are whisked away quietly and never seen.

The trouble with running from reality is that one day it will catch up with us, and the question is: *What then?* What does happen when you die? Shakespeare described death as an "undiscovered country" from which no traveller returns. So how can anyone possibly know for sure what happens?

But there is one person who knows for certain what lies beyond the grave and that is God himself. And in the Bible God reveals the truth about life and death to us. Not only that, but in Jesus, God has provided *the solution to death*. Jesus came "so that by his death he might break the power of him who holds the power of death—that is, the devil—and free those who all their lives were held in slavery by their fear of death" (Hebrews 2 v 14-15).

If we are those who trust in Jesus we have the answer to death. We can face it and think and talk about it and have no need to fear it, because we believe in the one who has destroyed it.

We may, however, still have plenty of questions.

What exactly does happen when we die? Where will I be five minutes later? What will become of our bodies? How can I be sure? What will happen on the day of judgment? Will there be rewards for believers? What will life be like in eternity? How do we cope with bereavement? Will we see our loved ones again?

It is to answer these and many more questions about death from the Bible that this book is written.

Chapter 1

Why is death such a problem?

For most people death is a scary prospect. For some it is fear of the unknown; for others it's the awareness that death makes life so meaningless. One journalist, Tom Chivers, wrote:

I'm terrified of death; my own, my loved ones, everyone's ... 100 years after my death, no-one will really know who I was. Do you even know your great-grandparents' names?

For some their fear is that death is the end. Larry King, the former CNN broadcaster, said: "My biggest fear is death, because I don't think I'm going anywhere".

But the Bible says the reason that we all fear death is precisely the opposite. Death is *not* the end. We are going somewhere, all of us, and unless we are trusting in Jesus we have everything to fear.

Hebrews 9 v 27 says "Man is destined to die once and after that to face judgment." People may not like to admit it, but deep down we all have a sneaking suspicion that the grave will not be the final word, and that one day justice will be done to us and to the whole world. This inner sense of a coming judgment is confirmed and brought into sharp focus by the Bible—nowhere quite as starkly as in the last book of the Bible.

> Then I saw a great white throne and him who was seated on it. The earth and the heavens fled from his presence, and there was no place for them. And I saw the dead, great and small, standing before the throne, and books were opened. Another book was opened, which is the book of life. The dead were judged according to what they had done as recorded in the books. The sea gave up the dead that were in it, and death and Hades gave up the dead that were in them, and each person was judged according to what they had done. Then death and Hades were thrown into the lake of fire. The lake of fire is the second death. Anyone whose name was not found written in the book of life, was thrown into the lake of fire.
>
> *Revelation 20 v 11-15*

The passage begins with the words: *Then I saw...* As we look over John's shoulder at what God revealed to him, we are given a window into what lies ahead. It is revealed to us so that we can prepare for it.

The courtroom

The heavenly scene appears to be a courtroom, but with some unusual features.

> Then I saw a great white throne and him who was seated on it. The earth and the heavens fled from his presence, and there was no place for them.
>
> *Verse 11*

The first thing that catches John's eye is a huge white throne. It's not what you find in a normal courtroom. A judge usually sits on what is called a bench but is more often than not a chair—definitely not on a throne. But this court is being held in the throne room of God. Seated on the throne is Almighty God, the Creator and Judge of all people. That the throne is great tells us that God's power, majesty and authority are great. The whiteness of the throne tells us that God is completely holy and pure.

The timing of the heavenly court is shown by the detail in v 11 that "The earth and the heavens fled from his presence, and there was no place for them". This court session will take place when Jesus returns and this present age comes to an end, making way for the new heavens and the new earth.

The accused

But as he looks, John sees not just God on his throne, but those who are standing before him. And what a sight it is:

> And I saw the dead, great and small, standing
> before the throne'.   *Verse 12*

Picture that. *Every* person who has *ever* lived standing before the enormous white throne. Billions of people. Great and small, rich and poor, the powerful and the oppressed. The great sprawling mass of humanity standing before their Creator. It is an awe-inspiring scene.

But this is not just a story in a book—because you will be there, and so will I. We will be there not as disembodied souls, but physically raised from the dead.

> The sea gave up the dead that were in it, and
> Death and Hades gave up the dead that were in
> them.   *Verse 13*

It doesn't matter how people died; everyone will be raised to life for this end-time court appearance. It doesn't matter whether they were buried, cremated or lost at sea—all will be raised.

This idea of a final resurrection of all people is not just something we find in the last book of the Bible. In the Old Testament the prophet Daniel prophesied that: "Multitudes who sleep in the dust of the earth will awake; some to everlasting life, others to shame and everlasting contempt." (Daniel 12 v 2). The apostle Paul teaches that: "there will be a resurrection of both the righteous and the wicked" (Acts 24 v 15). And Jesus himself states very clearly that: "A time is coming when all who are in their graves will hear his voice and come out" (John 5 v 28).

This is where history is heading. History isn't going endlessly round in circles—it's heading towards this final day of reckoning. It was Bertrand Russell who famously said: "When I die I shall rot", but Christians know that this is just wishful thinking. Death is not the end. We will all be raised from death to appear in this heavenly courtroom.

Is this really going to happen?

It's interesting that so many people appear to have a deep-seated feeling that one day justice will be done. We cannot imagine a universe in which those who have done evil will just get away with it. This universal inner sense that justice will one day be done is God-given and confirms the clear testimony of the Bible. But the ultimate proof is the resurrection of Jesus Christ.

As Paul says in Acts 17 v 31, God "has set a day when he will judge the world with justice by the man he has appointed. He has given proof of this to everyone by raising him from the dead."

The last days have already been set in motion by the resurrection of Jesus Christ.

The trial

Courtroom dramas make for good television viewing, but it's not quite so entertaining to find yourself featuring in one—especially when you are the defendant. Each of us will be on trial before the God who made us:

And I saw the dead, great and small, standing before the throne, and books were opened. An-

other book was opened, which is the book of life.
The dead were judged according to what they
had done as recorded in the books.   *Verse 12*

In John's vision there are two sets of books.

1. The books of deeds

First, the books of deeds: "The dead were judged according to what they had done as recorded in the books" (v 12) and "each person was judged according to what they had done."

The other day my wife found our two-year-old son in the living-room, his trousers soaked through, standing in a pool of pee, our attempts at potty-training looking rather pathetic.

My wife asked him: "Have you peed in your pants?" He looked at her and without missing a beat replied: "No, daddy did it!" You don't have to teach a two-year-old to pass the buck, and as adults we instinctively do the same when confronted with wrong in our lives.

But in these books is recorded everything we have ever done. We need to bear in mind that this is a part of the Bible which uses symbolism to represent reality. The books symbolise God's memory, in which absolutely *nothing* is missing.

Perhaps if God had given this vision today rather than in the 1st century, instead of books he may have pictured that record as a video of your life. Imagine that being projected onto a huge screen on that last day, with all the people you've ever known in this life watching with you. What rating do you think your film would be given by the censors?

All our secrets. All those things which we have now long forgotten. There would be so much of which we would be ashamed. If the video was posted on your Facebook site, how many friends would you have this time next week?

In TV detective shows a recurring challenge is the need to get enough evidence to prove someone's guilt. Sometimes a case collapses because there's not enough evidence. But if the charge at the final judgment is failing to love God and your neighbour as God commands, how long would it take to establish your guilt? How long would the film need to run before we'd say: "Okay, spare us the rest. I plead guilty!"?

The trial will be *totally* just and fair because all the evidence will be there. There'll be no rough justice, because judgment will not be based on reputation or appearance or family connections. And God knows *all the facts*. Not only what happened, but what was in our hearts. He knows all the circumstances and mitigating factors in full. Unlike us, his judgments are based on knowing all the facts in intimate detail. In the words of Romans 2 v 6: *"God will give to each person according to what he has done."*

Sometimes people say things like: "I'm basically a good person", or "I'm much better than many others". But based on such a judgment, who could possibly walk away from that court a free man or woman?

2. The book of life

But wonderfully verse 12 says: "Another book was opened, which is the book of life". This book comes up six times in Revelation. In 21 v 27 it's called "the Lamb's book of life". According to 20 v 15 this book records not deeds but names—the names of God's people. It's a register of the citizens of the heavenly city. They alone escape the fiery fate at the end of verse 15.

There is only one way to walk free from that heavenly courtroom, and that is to have your name in that book of life. Other verses in Revelation tell us how to get our name into it. 1 v 5: "To him who loves us and has freed us from our sins by his blood." 7 v 14 "They have washed their robes and made them white in the blood of the Lamb". This book isn't a Who's Who of the rich and famous. It is a record of all those who have put their trust in Jesus and his death for their forgiveness.

It's not clear from this passage whether or not these people also have their deeds recorded in the other books. If so, the books may contain plenty of good deeds, which are the fruit of a living faith and would be a public confirmation on that last day of our faith in Jesus.

Perhaps in those books there would be no record of any of our wrongdoing, since Christ has paid for it all; or maybe it would be recorded to show the wonder of God's grace to us. What we do know for certain is that "There is now no condemnation for those who are in Christ Jesus" (Romans 8 v 1).

Is your name listed in that book of life? In the end, wherever else your name appears is of no consequence.

Your name may end up in the newspapers, or on the side of a company building, or even in history books. But none of this matters if it is not found in the book of life on that last day.

By contrast, your name may never make any impact in this world. It may be quickly forgotten once you've gone. But none of this matters either—if your name is written in the book of life! If it is, then that is a cause for daily thanksgiving and joy. As Jesus said to his disciples: "Rejoice that your names are written in heaven" (Luke 10 v 20).

The sentence

It really matters that our names are written there when we consider the sentence with which the trial concludes:

> Then death and Hades were thrown into the lake of fire. The lake of fire is the second death. Anyone whose name was not found written in the book of life, was thrown into the lake of fire.   *Verse 14*

There is no long-drawn-out debate, no court of appeal, no second chance. The sentence of the court is final and swiftly executed. If anyone's name is not found written in the book of life, they are thrown into the lake of fire. The lake of fire is mentioned three times in v 14-15 for emphasis. It is also referred to there as *"the second death"*.

The Bible speaks of two deaths. The first death is what we refer to as death; that is, the end of our life here on earth. The second death is this fate in the lake of fire for those whose names are not written in the book of life.

Fire is a picture of God's judgment. The lake of fire is the place where, back in v 10, we read that the devil is also thrown to be "tormented day and night for ever and ever". It is to live on under God's judgment in a condition where, according to 14 v 11, there is "no rest day or night". It is what Jesus often referred to as a place of weeping and gnashing of teeth. The lake of fire presumably symbolises God's judgment rather than being literal, and medieval artists have not done us any favours by letting their imaginations run riot in trying to paint this scene for us. But the reality it does symbolise, of ongoing eternal existence under God's judgment, is no less horrific.

"I'm not afraid of death" people sometimes say who have no time for God. And perhaps they are not. But death is not the biggest problem. The problem is what lies beyond. Not to be afraid of the second death is sheer folly. Other people are afraid of dying because they fear the unknown, but there is even more reason to be afraid of death once you do know what lies beyond.

Comforting?

A Bible passage like this can be a source of much heartache for those who have been bereaved. It's understandable that we fear for our loved ones who have died and who, as far as we know, didn't trust in Jesus. But who knows where someone stood before God at the moment of death? Some people really do turn to God in their final hours. We need to leave them in God's hands. What matters now is those of us who are still living and who do still have time to prepare for this final appointment.

For those who are followers of Jesus, this vision of future reality is an encouragement to us to persevere in faith. Our names are written in the book of life. In just a little while we will be enjoying what Revelation chapters 21-22 go on to describe, and which we will look at in the final chapter of this book. This is where Christians are heading, so whatever the cost, however much of a struggle we have with sin and temptation and opposition, this is why we must hang in there and keep going.

When we're tempted to give up and swap sides—when we're aware that we are drifting away from the gospel— we need to look through the window of this vision and remind ourselves of this defining future reality.

But for those who are not followers of Jesus, this trailer of what lies ahead is a gracious warning from God and an invitation to receive God's forgiveness in Christ while there is still time.

On a beach in Indonesia on Boxing Day, 26th December in 2004, a 12-year-old Saudi boy called Youssuf, who was on holiday with his family, was looking through his binoculars at the sea. One account recorded that suddenly: "he yelled 'tsunami!' as hard as he could, but nobody believed him. Tragically, the boy's mother and 4-year old brother were swept away to their deaths".

The apostle John is looking through his binoculars and has seen what happens at the end of time. He is yelling: *"Judgment is coming"*. We do well to believe him, and, if we believe him, to warn others. But sadly many in our world are like the people described in Genesis 19. In that account of the destruction of the city of Sodom we read in v 14 that Lot warned his sons-in-law:

"Hurry and get out of this place, because the LORD is about to destroy the city!" But it goes on: "his sons-in-law thought he was joking." They ignored him and they perished.

God is not joking. This is for real and people ignore the warning at their peril.

When you learn to drive in the UK, one of the things they teach you is about how to deal with intersections where there is a large rectangular box of yellow grid lines painted in the middle on the road. The rule: *Don't enter the box until your exit is clear.* That is also wise advice about death.

One day each of us will enter another box and be lowered into the ground or cremated. Before that happens, we do well to make sure our exit is clear into the glorious future of Revelation chapters 21 – 22.

But as to when that day of death will come, none of us knows. That is why the Bible urges that "now is the time of God's favour, now is the day of salvation" (2 Corinthians 6 v 2).

Should we pray for the dead?

We can certainly give thanks to God for our loved ones who have died, but the Bible nowhere encourages us to pray for the dead because there is actually no point in doing so.

When someone dies, either they go to be with the Lord or are separated from him, and nothing we do after their death can alter their state or destiny. The believer is "with Christ, which is better by far" (Philippians 1 v 23), and so has nothing lacking for which they need us to pray.

The unbeliever has no more opportunity to respond to the gospel once they have died, so praying for them would also not achieve anything. This is why the Bible is so urgent about what we do with the gospel in this life, while there is still time. We should be thankful for the lives of those who have died, but we must trust them to God and be devoted to praying for the living.

By contrast, the Roman Catholic Church teaches that the great majority of believers go to purgatory when they die—an intermediate stage where they are supposedly purified by fire to fit them for heaven. Believers still alive on earth are thought to be able to help those in purgatory by praying for them and obtaining remission of sin ("indulgences") from the Church.

This teaching is without any foundation in the Bible. It also goes against the clear teaching of Scripture that when a person puts their faith in Christ they are from that moment justified, put right with God, fully accepted by him. The assurance we have is that "since we have been justified through faith, we have peace with God through our Lord Jesus Christ" (Romans 5 v 1).

The wonder of the gospel is that because Christ suffered for our sins, we don't have to (1 Peter 3 v 18).

Chapter 2

How can I be sure?

We never know how we will cope with death until we actually face its brutal reality. We may be full of confident answers to others in their moment of need. But then the phone rings and someone starts by asking: "are you sitting down?" Or you visit the doctor for some test results and he says to you: "It's bad news, I'm afraid—the worst possible kind."

It is not unusual for all our confident belief to slip away at that moment as we are dazed by disbelief and the question: *Why?*

There were two sisters who lost their beloved brother. Neither could understand why. And when they asked their question to the person who could have prevented it, this was his reply:

Jesus said: "I am the resurrection and the life. The one who believes in me will live, even though they dies, and whoever lives by believing in me will never die. Do you believe this?" *John 11 v 25*

It's a good question. What would you answer? If you are a follower of Jesus, do you believe this? Do you believe it enough for it to make a difference when the day comes that a loved one dies, or that you yourself get out of bed for the last time?

Do you believe it enough to tell others about what Jesus has promised? And if you aren't a follower of Jesus, can your worldview cope with death? What hope do your beliefs or philosophy offer you in the face of death? These words of Jesus are either the greatest con ever or the defeat of our greatest enemy, death itself. The raising from death to life of a man called Lazarus, recorded in John 11, assures us it is the latter. Take the time to read the whole of John chapter 11 in your Bible before you read on.

The purpose of the miracle (v 1-16)
God's glory

Jesus is east of the Jordan when news is brought to him that Lazarus, the brother of Mary and Martha, is ill:

> When he heard this, Jesus said, "This illness will
> not end in death. No, it is for God's glory so that
> God's Son may be glorified through it."   *Verse 4*

The miracle will reveal God's glory as his power is displayed, and it will bring glory to God the Father and the Son of God. Jesus makes the same point to Martha, just before he does the miracle:

> "Did I not tell you that if you believe you will see
> the glory of God?"   *verse 40*

So one purpose of this miracle is to reveal God's glory—in this case his power over death.

The miracles of Jesus are an absolute gift if you're teaching children in Sunday School. The accounts are dramatic, visual, and lend themselves to fun role-play and making all manner of things out of cardboard. "'Who's going to be Lazarus? Let's wrap them in toilet paper, and this cupboard can be the tomb!" But with adults there is perhaps a tendency to focus on the teaching of Jesus instead. The Sermon on the Mount can seem safer ground than someone being raised from the dead—it's more plausible, more acceptable to the skeptic—but adults also need to learn these true stories of Jesus' miracles, because God's glory is revealed not just in Jesus' words but in his mighty works.

Our faith

Jesus says the purpose of the miracle is also for our faith. In 20 v 31 we are told that the miracles are recorded "that you may believe that Jesus is the Messiah, the Son of God". The miracles provide a foundation for faith, reasons to believe, as we see in chapter 11. Just after the Lord Jesus raises Lazarus, we read:

> Therefore many of the Jews who had come to visit Mary, and had seen what Jesus did, put their faith in him.   *verse 45*

They came to faith on the basis of what they *saw* Jesus do. But this miracle is not just for the benefit of those who don't yet believe in Jesus, but also for those who do. Speaking to the disciples, Jesus said:

> "Lazarus is dead, and for your sake I am glad I
> was not there, so that you may believe." *Verse 14*

Surely the disciples already believe! Well, they do and they don't. They do, but their faith in Jesus needs to develop and grow, mature and deepen. It needs stretching and strengthening.

We see this very clearly in the two sisters, Martha and Mary. They both say exactly the same thing to Jesus in v 21 and v 32: "Lord, if you had been here, my brother would not have died". They both believe that if Jesus had arrived in time, he could have healed Lazarus. They believe—but they don't believe he can raise Lazarus to life now that he is dead.

In v 39 when Jesus says: "Take away the stone" from the tomb, Martha tries to stop him, saying: "By this time there is a bad odour, for he has been there four days." She believes, but her faith has limits. Martha says in v 27: "I believe that you are the Messiah, the Son of God, who was to come into the world", and so she does, but she has a limited view of what that means—a Messiah who can heal the sick, but not a Messiah who can raise the dead.

This perspective on faith should make us ask two questions: *Do I have faith in Christ or not?* And if I do believe in him, *is my faith growing?* The miracles of Jesus serve to bring people to faith, but also to stretch the faith of believers. Faith is like a muscle. It needs to grow and be strengthened, and for that to happen it needs to be stretched, put under pressure, tested. So you believe Jesus is the Christ, the Son of God, the resurrection and the life? What can your Jesus do? Can he raise the dead? Do you believe that? Do you believe it enough for it to make a difference when you are facing death yourself or when a loved one dies?

To prepare us for that time, God will put us in situations to stretch our faith and make it grow. He does this because he loves us. We read in verse 5: "Jesus loved Martha and her sister and Lazarus. So when he heard that Lazarus was ill, he stayed where he was two more days." If he loved them, why the delay? Why let Lazarus die? He did it to stretch and strengthen their faith. Faith does not grow in the sunshine. It grows by being tested. He delayed out of love for them.

Love that tests

When we're going through hard times—at work, at home, with ill-health—we may well ask with frustration: "Why the delay? Why doesn't God intervene if he loves me?" Have you ever thought that God might be allowing this to happen *precisely because he loves you* and wants to strengthen and deepen your faith?

The ultimate test of faith is death itself, when one day you are told you have a month to live, or you get a phone call saying your mother or father, or your husband or wife, has just died. At that moment, and in the days that follow, you will need a faith that is strong and has deep roots. But such faith does not spring up overnight. It is the result of years of being tested and matured by other lesser challenges and hardships. The trials that you are going through at the moment are for your good, so that your faith will grow and be able to cope with death when it comes.

There is a parallel in weight training. To quote the former bodybuilder, Arnold Schwarzenegger:

> *The last three or four repetitions is what makes the muscle grow. This area of pain divides the champion from someone else who is not a champion. That's what most people lack, having the guts to go on and just say they'll go through the pain no matter what happens.*

Muscles grow through painful testing—so does faith.

The significance of the miracle (v 17-37)

In verses 25-26 Jesus says to Martha:

> "I am the resurrection and the life. The one who believes in me will live, even though they die; and whoever lives by believing in me will never die."

The first bit, *I am the resurrection*, is explained by Jesus in the rest of v 25: *The one who believes in me will live, even though they die*—that is dies physically. As "the resurrection", Jesus promises life beyond the grave for those who trust in him.

The theme song of *Fame*—the film, TV series and musical—declared, "Fame, I'm gonna live forever". That is not what Jesus is talking about. Jesus is promising life with God beyond the grave, and ultimately physical resurrection to a new life in the age to come.

And this is not just *resuscitation* either. Resuscitation involves being revived but then eventually having to die again. By contrast, Jesus is promising life after death—the defeat of death. But note that this isn't just automatic. This life beyond the grave is only for "the one who believes in me".

As a church minister, before a funeral I meet up with the family to talk through the service and find out about the person who has died. Time and again the family will say things like: "At least Fred is now at peace and in a better place", even when Fred had nothing whatsoever to do with Jesus when he was alive. It's wishful thinking. It's assuming that everyone qualifies for what Jesus promises, regardless of whether or not they have trusted in him. It's desperately sad because it's wrong. "I am the resurrection and the life. The one who believes in me will live, even though they die."

I am the life

The second part of Jesus' claim is *I am the life*, which Jesus then explains in verse 26: *whoever lives and believes in me will never die*. In what sense do those who believe in him never die?

Physically, of course, followers of Jesus die like everyone else, and at some point Lazarus himself would die again and have another funeral. But the Bible talks about the "second death" which is the "lake of fire" (Revelation 20 v 14; 21 v 8). The second death of eternal judgment—hell—is a much bigger problem than the first death. But those who trust in Jesus will never die in that sense. Someone has put it this way: *If you've been* born only once, you will die twice; but if you've been born twice [that is, physically, and spiritually through being born again], you'll only die once.

But why does Jesus say "whoever lives and believes in me"? Surely it's self-evident that you need to be physically alive to believe in Jesus. Probably what Jesus means is everyone who lives, not just physically, but spiritually through having eternal life. For those who trust in Jesus eternal life begins now.

In John 5 v 24 Jesus says, *I tell you the truth, whoever hears my word and believes him who sent me has eternal life and will not be condemned; he has crossed over from death to life.* If you believe in Jesus, you have already crossed over from death to life. Without this eternal life now we are just existing, just filling in time on the planet, no better than cows in the field. Jesus is offering both life before death, and life after death.

The evidence for the miracle (v 38-44)

The evidence to support Jesus' claim is very convincing.

Lazarus was most definitely dead. Look at the explicit expressions—v 39 speaks of *Martha, the sister of the dead man* and v 44 refers to *the dead man*. Look at the time in the tomb—v 17 says, *On his arrival, Jesus found that Lazarus had already been in the tomb for four days.* Lazarus was dead and buried. Not only had he been in there four days, but verse 44 also mentions that his hands and feet had been bound with strips of linen and his face wrapped with a cloth. Look at the many mourners—v 19 says *"many Jews had come to Martha and Mary to com-*

fort them in the loss of their brother". The intense grief of the mourners in v 33 makes clear that there was no doubt in any of their minds that he was dead. Look at the nasty niffs—in v 39 Martha says, *by this time there is a bad odour, for he has been there four days*. Or as the old Authorized Version puts it, *Lord, by this time he stinketh!* Decomposition in the hot climate of Palestine would have been rapid. Lazarus was most definitely dead.

But Lazarus was also most definitely raised.

> Jesus called in a loud voice, "Lazarus, come out!" The dead man came out, his hands and feet wrapped with strips of linen, and a cloth around his face.   *Verse 43*

Someone has speculated that Jesus said: "*Lazarus*, come out" because if he hadn't specified his name, then all the dead in the area would have emerged from their tombs, such is the power of Jesus' command. It's a nice idea.

Look at the enemy reaction.

> Then the chief priests and the Pharisees called a meeting of the Sanhedrin. "What are we accomplishing?" they asked. "Here is this man performing many signs. If we let him go on like this, everyone will believe in him."   *Verses 47-48*

If even his enemies acknowledged the miracle, that's pretty strong evidence. And how could they deny it? A large crowd had witnessed it and verse 45 records that many of the Jews who had seen it believed in him. This was a public event.

Look at the thanksgiving celebration.

Six days before the Passover, Jesus came to Bethany, where Lazarus lived, whom Jesus had raised from the dead. Here a dinner was given in Jesus' honour. Martha served, while Lazarus was among those reclining at the table with him.   *12 v 1-2*

What a dinner that must have been with Lazarus actually there eating with them. Lots of jokes no doubt at Lazarus' expense—"Dig in Laz, you haven't eaten for days" and the like!

Look at the tourist attraction.

Meanwhile a large crowd of Jews found out that Jesus was there and came, not only because of him but also to see Lazarus, whom he had raised from the dead. So the chief priests made plans to kill Lazarus as well, for on account of him many of the Jews were going over to Jesus and believing in him.   *12 v 9-11*

All the evidence points in one direction—Lazarus was definitely raised from the dead. When someone claims to be the resurrection and the life, and then raises to life someone who's been dead and buried for four days, we'd be fools to ignore him.

Jesus said: "I am the resurrection and the life. He who believes in me will live, even though they die, and whoever lives by believing in me will never die. Do you believe this?"

If you are not a follower of Jesus, this invitation to put your trust in Jesus goes out to you even today. Who else can tackle death for you?

And if you are a follower of Jesus, do you actually believe what Jesus is saying here? Do you believe it enough to tell others about it? Will you allow God to strengthen your faith through testing times? Will you see that testing—painful and bewildering as it may be when you go through it—as loving preparation for the ultimate test of faith: when your loved ones, and you yourself, are called to walk through the valley of the shadow of death. Will you put your hand in his and trust him to walk with you through that darkest valley and bring you out safely on the other side?

Are ghosts for real?

A ghost is a supposed apparition of a dead person. Twice the disciples mistook Jesus for a ghost or spirit (Mark 6 v 49; Luke 24 v 37). Jesus didn't in either case deny the existence of such spiritual beings, but rather, just insisted he was not a ghost—just himself.

There are spiritual beings active in this world—angels

serving God and his people (Hebrews 1 v 13-14); and spiritual forces of evil serving the devil (Ephesians 6 v 12), who feature in the Gospels as demons and unclean spirits.

In addition to such spiritual beings, when people die they live on as spirits, awaiting the physical resurrection. But these spirits of dead people go either to be with the Lord or to a place separated from him (see Luke 16 v 26-31). They are not left on earth to wander around and to haunt places as ghosts or poltergeists, even when the deceased person died young or unprepared or wasn't properly buried.

There are only two biblical examples of the spirits of dead people appearing on earth. One is when Moses and Elijah appeared with Jesus when he was transfigured on the mountain (Mark 9 v 4-5). The other was when the spirit of Samuel appeared to Saul, who used a medium, the witch of Endor, to summon him (1 Samuel 28 v 11-15).

Jesus' encounter as the Son of God with these prophets is a unique experience that we should not expect to be repeated or to seek for ourselves. And what Saul did in trying to contact the dead through a medium is specifically forbidden and condemned in the Bible in the severest possible terms (see Leviticus 19 v 31; 20 v 6). Seeking contact with spirits in this way may actually expose a person to evil spirits masquerading as the spirit of the deceased person. Scripture warns us that the devil is a deceiver (Revelation 12 v 9) who disguises himself as an angel of light (2 Corinthians 11 v 14) in order to draw us away from God.

Chapter 3

What will happen to my body?

A few days ago I began to have a sore throat, a fever and swollen glands, so I thought I'd try a bit of self-diagnosis and went online to do a search on my symptoms. *Big mistake!*

I read the list of nasty, debilitating and deadly diseases with a growing terror: tonsillitis, glandular fever, Hodgkin's disease. It turned to be nothing serious, but it did remind me of how fragile our lives are. The human body is a phenomenal piece of equipment, run by what is still the world's most powerful supercomputer, but it is also frighteningly vulnerable. There are a million and one diseases which could kill you, and one day one of them will, unless you get run over by a bus before then.

It doesn't matter how well you look after yourself or how much you go to the gym. Bruce Lee, the martial arts expert, was able to do over 60 one-arm pull-ups and had the reputation of being the fittest man alive. But then at the age of 32 he fell into a coma in his Hong Kong apartment and died very suddenly. You may have a fantastically healthy diet and never smoke or drink, but one day your body is going to conk out. *What then?*

Fast-forward in your mind to your own funeral. On that day, what does the future hold for you? Some think death is the end. Others think life goes on in some sense beyond the grave. But Christians don't fall into either category. We don't think death is the end, but we don't think either that life just goes on in the same way.

Christians believe something completely outrageous and unique. One of the earliest statements of faith is called the Apostles' Creed. This is how it ends:

> I believe in the forgiveness of sins, the resurrection of the body and the life everlasting.

Christians don't just have a vague hope that life will continue in some spiritual form after death, or even that they will "go to heaven" in some mystical way. Christians believe in the resurrection of the body and the life everlasting. 1 Corinthians 15 is all about resurrection. In it the apostle Paul argues that the bodily resurrection of Christians will happen and that it does matter, but his starting point is not *our* resurrection but that of Jesus Christ. He begins there because that historical event and our future resurrection as believers are inseparably connected. We're going to look at three aspects of Christ's resurrection and the implications for us.

The nature of Christ's resurrection

Now, brothers and sisters, I want to remind you of the gospel I preached to you, which you received and on which you have taken your stand. By this gospel you are saved, if you hold firmly to the word I preached to you. Otherwise, you have believed in vain. For what I received I passed on to you as of first importance: that Christ died for our sins according to the Scriptures, that he was buried, that he was raised on the third day according to the Scriptures, and that he appeared to Cephas, and then to the Twelve. After that, he appeared to more than five hundred of the brothers and sisters at the same time, most of whom are still living, though some have fallen asleep. Then he appeared to James, then to all the apostles, and last of all he appeared to me also, as to one abnormally born.

For I am the least of the apostles and do not even deserve to be called an apostle, because I persecuted the church of God.

1 Corinthians 15 v 1-9

Christ was raised bodily...

In v 3-5 the apostle Paul writes that Christ died, was buried, was raised and appeared. Notice the continuity. The person who was raised and who appeared is the same person who died and was buried. A body was crucified and buried, and the same body was raised and then appeared. The tomb was empty. Jesus' resurrection was not just a mystical, spiritual affair as some people suggest. It was a physical event. The appearances to the people listed in v 5-9 were not those of a ghost or spirit, but rather, it was Jesus Christ raised bodily from the grave.

In Luke 24 v 37, when the risen Jesus appeared to his disciples, they were scared stiff and thought it was a ghost. But Jesus reassured them: "Look at my hands and my feet. It is I myself! Touch me and see; a ghost does not have flesh and bones, as you see I have." And to prove the point, he ate a piece of fish right in front of them.

... so we will be raised bodily

The consequence for the Christian is that we too will be raised bodily from death. One of the key words in 1 Corinthians 15 is the Greek word *nekros,* meaning the dead or a corpse. When it talks about the dead being raised, it is talking about resurrection of the physical corpse from death to life.

In fact Paul later addresses the specific question of what *kind* of bodies we will have when we are raised: "But someone will ask, 'How are the dead raised? With what kind of body will they come?'" (verse 35). The answer he gives is that there will both continuity and transformation of our bodies.

The risen Jesus still had the nail wounds in his hands and feet and side. But that doesn't mean you will have your C-section or appendix scar for all eternity. Jesus' scars remained to establish for us without doubt that it really was him who was raised. They will be a glorious reminder to us of the cost of us being in the new creation.

Will we be the age we were when we died? Presumably not, but rather, in our prime. Will we be the same basic body shape? What if you've struggled all your life with being too short, too fat, too thin? Suffice to say, we don't have all the answers, but none of us will have body issues in the age to come!

Christ's resurrection has established the pattern that we as Christians will follow. That means we're not talking about some disembodied existence where we float around on clouds. We're talking about empty graves and the resurrection of you as a person.

The fact of Christ's resurrection

But did Christ's resurrection really happen? The first 11 verses point us to two bits of historical evidence.

The empty tomb: In v 4 it says "that he was buried, that he was raised on the third day … and that he appeared to Cephas [Peter]." If the person who was buried is then raised to life and appears to people, you're left with an empty tomb. The body isn't in there any more because it's walking around outside. The sign outside the tomb has to be changed back from "engaged" to "vacant".

In Luke 24 v 5, when the women arrive at the tomb, they find the stone rolled away and two angels standing there who say to them: "Why do you look for the living among the dead? He is not here; he has risen!" And in verse 23, the two disciples on the road to Emmaus relate how the women went to the tomb "but didn't find his body".

If anyone at any time after the resurrection of Christ had been able to produce Jesus' body—his corpse—Christianity would have sunk without trace and that would have been the end of it. But there was no corpse because the body had been raised to life. The empty tomb is a powerful piece of evidence. You can go to Red Square in Moscow and see Lenin's embalmed body on public display. Followers of Bruce Lee go to visit his grave in Seattle's Lake View Cemetery, where the remains of his super-fit body are interred. Followers of Muhammed go on pilgrimage to the Mosque of the Prophet in Medina, where the prophet is buried. But followers of Jesus Christ going to the Garden Tomb in Jerusalem find just an empty grave.

The appearances: The second piece of evidence is Christ's appearances listed in v 5-8. It's an impressive catalogue. He appeared to individuals, to groups of people, and on one occasion to more than 500 people, most of whom were still alive when Paul was writing—the implication being: *go and ask them about it yourself if you've got any doubts.*

The impact of one of these appearances is really striking; namely, the appearance of Christ to Paul—v 8

> Last of all he appeared to me also, as to one abnormally born. For I am the least of the apostles and do not even deserve to be called an apostle, because I persecuted the church of God. But by the grace of God I am what I am, and his grace to me was not without effect. No, I worked harder than all of them—yet not I, but the grace of God that was with me. Whether, then, it is I or they, this is what we preach, and this is what you believed.

What a transformation! Paul had been having Christians

arrested and put to death, but then Christ appeared to him one day on the road to Damascus. Paul stopped dead in his tracks and his life was never the same again. From that moment on, he was dedicated to working tirelessly to spread the message of Jesus, preaching the faith he had been trying to destroy. It was a conviction he ended up dying for.

That Jesus really was raised from death means that Christian belief in the resurrection of the body is not wishful thinking. It is built on a rock-solid historical foundation. We can say the final line of the Apostles' Creed with conviction: "I believe in the resurrection of the body and the life everlasting", because we are convinced that the middle part is true, which says that Jesus Christ was "crucified, dead and buried, and on the third day he rose again from the dead".

The importance of Christ's resurrection

Which is the biggest day for Christians at Easter? Good Friday, remembering the death of Christ? Or Easter Sunday, remembering his resurrection? Intriguingly, Christians have adopted as their central symbol the cross and not the empty tomb, and rightly so because it is only through the death of Jesus that we are forgiven and put right with God. But Christians sometimes make the mistake of neglecting Jesus' resurrection, as if it's not really that important. 1 Corinthians 15 puts Christ's resurrection back on the map.

In v 1-2 Paul writes:

Now, brothers and sisters, I want to remind you of

the gospel I preached to you, which you received and on which you have taken your stand. By this gospel you are saved, if you hold firmly to the word I preached to you. Otherwise, you have be-lieved in vain.

To be saved, a person has to believe, and continue to believe, the gospel message—but what exactly is this gospel message? Verses 3-5 tell us:

For what I received I passed on to you as of first importance: that Christ died for our sins according to the Scriptures, that he was buried, that he was raised on the third day according to the Scriptures, and that he appeared to Cephas [Peter], and then to the Twelve.

Together with the death of Christ, the resurrection of Christ is of first importance, foretold in the Old Testa-ment—an essential part of the gospel message. If you don't believe in the resurrection of Christ, Paul says *you have believed in vain*. Paul wrote this because the Christians at Corinth would not have had a problem with making little or nothing of the resurrection, so why is Paul making such a big deal about it? The clue is in v 12.

But if it is preached that Christ has been raised from the dead, how can some of you say that there is no resurrection of the dead? If there is no resurrection of the dead, then not even Christ has been raised. And if Christ has not been raised, our preaching is useless and so is your faith.

The church at Corinth had no problem with the resurrection of Christ. They believed it. What they *did* struggle with was the bodily resurrection of believers. In fact v 12 says that some were denying that the dead are raised. But if you deny bodily resurrection, you're denying the bodily resurrection of Christ as well, because the two go together. Deny one and you deny the other. The Corinthian Christians were being inconsistent and illogical. They wanted to hold on to the one (Christ's resurrection) but do away with the other (their own resurrection), but that is something we cannot do. If you are a Christian, then belief in your own bodily resurrection is non-negotiable.

Mad society

Why were some denying the resurrection of the body? For the same reasons we are tempted to deny it today. First, because of the surrounding culture. Greek philosophy believed in the immortality of the soul but rejected completely the resurrection of the body. Perhaps without being aware of it, the Corinthians let their beliefs be shaped by the surrounding culture. Or perhaps they deliberately *changed* their beliefs to make them more acceptable in Greek society.

As Christians today we need to beware the influence of the culture in which we live. If you say you believe in bodily resurrection, people are going to laugh in your face, and think up 101 difficult questions for you, ranging from cremation to whether there will be bathrooms in heaven! It's tempting to retreat to a more acceptable position—of life continuing in just some spiritual sense, as many non-Christians believe. At funerals a poem is sometimes read called *Do not weep*:

> Do not stand by my grave and weep
>> I am not there, I do not sleep,
>> I am the thousand winds that blow ...
> Do not stand by my grave and cry,
>> I am not there, I did not die.

Many people find this sort of vague mysticism acceptable, so Christians who say that they just believe in "some sort of hereafter" fit in okay. But that is not biblical Christianity.

But we can end up in error not just by following our society but by reacting against it. Our culture worships the body. Just think of the place of sport, the obsession with fitness, the cosmetics industry, the advertising and botox. It's possible for Christians to react against that idolatry by dismissing the body and just focusing on the spirit. But we mustn't let culture call the tune, either by us following it or by reacting against it.

Bad theology

Second, there were also theological reasons why some at Corinth had turned their backs on the resurrection of the body. There's evidence elsewhere in the letter that some of them thought that through receiving the Spirit they had begun a form of angelic existence now—a life in which the body was unnecessary and would one day be destroyed. That may sound extreme, but here are three common errors which can leave us moving in a similar direction.

The first common mistake is *a focus on "now" rather than the age to come:* emphasising our present experience as Christians so much that we forget that the biblical centre of gravity is in the world to come, when God's people are bodily raised for life in the eternal kingdom of God. A gospel message which invites people to come to Jesus purely so he can sort their lives out, solve all their problems, give them purpose and help them fulfil their potential, is not biblical Christianity. It's more like a modern self-help scheme with a Christian label stuck on it.

A second mistake is *a focus on the soul rather than the whole person.* This heresy has a long history—certain 2nd-century sects taught that our souls are a "divine spark", trapped in the body and that salvation is the escape of the soul from the body to the heavenly realms above. A bishop called Irenaeus devoted much of his life to countering such teaching, but it seems to be making a comeback. Many Christians today think of their future purely in terms of "going to heaven" when they die—but that is sub-Christian—it's not the complete picture.

It *is* true that when a Christian dies, their spirit goes immediately to be with the Lord. And that is why, faced with death, Paul says in Philippians 1 v 23 that *to die and be with Christ is far better.* But that is just a temporary state. At Christ's return we will be raised bodily, and the resurrection body will be reunited with the spirit.

Christ's return is the trigger mechanism for that to happen and that is why the New Testament hardly ever speaks of looking forward to death. Instead the focus is Christ's return when we will experience the salvation of the whole person—spirit, soul and body (1 Thessalonians 5 v 23).

A third mistake is *a focus on me rather than the whole cosmos*. Sometimes as Christians our thoughts of salvation are too small. We think of salvation as just being about "me" going to be with the Lord for ever, and so we slip into thinking purely in terms of the soul. We wouldn't if we thought about salvation as the Bible does.

God's purposes are not just for you to be united with him, but for the renewal of *the whole material universe*. Salvation is going to be on a cosmic scale. Romans 8 v 21 says: "The creation itself will be liberated from its bondage to decay". In his vision in Revelation 21 v 1, John is shown a new heavens and a new earth, a renewed creation. The coming kingdom of God doesn't *do away* with the material world—it *redeems* it and *renews* it. We won't be forever twanging harps on clouds. We'll be enjoying life in resurrection bodies in a renewed material universe.

And all this flows from the resurrection of Christ. If you are not a follower of Jesus, you may until now have been happy in your belief that death is the end, or that life goes on in some mystical way. But what do you make of the resurrection of Jesus Christ? It throws a huge wrench into the works of those views. What will you do with that historical event? The empty tomb and the resurrection appearances are not going to go away. At the very least they deserve a closer look.

For those of us who are followers of Jesus, this passage calls us back to a confident faith in the resurrection of the body—your body. Do you believe in the resurrection of Christ? If so, you need to believe in your *own* resurrection, because it's going to happen. That is something to rejoice in and look forward to and live in the light of. It also means that life in the body now matters.

It should give us a renewed commitment to living godly lives. As Paul writes in v 34: "Come back to your senses as you ought, and stop sinning." Future resurrection means that what I do with my body matters, so I need to stop sinning.

It should also give us a renewed commitment to gospel work, as v 58 says: "Therefore, my dear brothers and sisters, stand firm. Let nothing move you. Always give yourselves fully to the work of the Lord, because you know that your labour in the Lord is not in vain."

One church where I worked used to get together with other churches every year on Easter Sunday morning and celebrate the resurrection of Christ at a sunrise service. The service was held outdoors in the middle of the city cemetery. As a minister, I'd buried a fair few people in that cemetery, some of whom were my friends. It is a powerful and moving experience to stand among the graves as the sun rises and to sing *Thine be the glory risen conquering Son, endless is the victory thou o'er death has won.*

We believe in the resurrection of the body and the life everlasting.

Cremation or burial?

Cremation in the Christian community is actually only a very recent development. Although cremation was practised by the Greeks and Romans, the early Christians insisted instead on burying their dead, and by the 5th century cremation had been abandoned throughout the Roman Empire due to Christian influence.

It was because of their belief in the resurrection of the body that Christians practised burial, following the pattern of Jesus' burial and resurrection. This was in contrast to the pagan belief that the body now had no further purpose and so might as well be destroyed. In the Bible, burning with fire has associations of pagan practice (the King of Edom in Amos 2 v 1; child sacrifice to Molech in 2 Kings 23 v 10) and God's judgment both now (Achan in Joshua 7 v 25) and in eternity (Mark 9 v 44, 48).

For these reasons, and given the Bible's view of the believer's body as a temple of the Holy Spirit, many Christians favour burial. Either way we should ensure that after death the body is treated with respect and dignity.

If a Christian in faith and good conscience chooses cremation, either for themselves or a loved one, perhaps because of concerns about land use or cost, they are not sinning. When all is said and done, the Bible nowhere explicitly condemns cremation, and when it comes to God raising the dead, it will make no difference whether the person was cremated or buried. In the history of the Church many martyrs have been burned, but they will not be at a disadvantage on the day of resurrection.

In the beginning God created everything out of nothing, and then made man from the dust of the earth, so raising a body from ashes is no problem to the all-powerful Creator. What ultimately matters is that we are those who believe in, and proclaim, the resurrection of the body and the life of the world to come.

Chapter 4

What will it be like to die?

In Shakespeare's *Hamlet* there's a famous scene in a graveyard. The grave diggers unearth some skulls, one of which turns out to be that of the court jester, Yorick, whom Hamlet knew.

Alas poor Yorick, I knew him Horatio; a fellow of infinite jest ... he hath borne me on his back a thousand times...

Hamlet reflects on how strange it is that we all come to this end, and that even Alexander the Great might become the bung in a beer-barrel, and "Imperious Caesar, dead and turn'd to clay, might stop a hole to keep the wind away." If death is the end, it makes everything so pointless, and that is one reason why for many death is such a taboo subject, the "elephant in the room", which we pretend is not there.

By contrast the Bible talks a lot about this particular elephant. It confronts head-on our biggest fear—the fear of death—and shows us how we can face it with confidence. John Newton was an 18th-century minister most famous now for his hymn *Amazing Grace*. He and his wife adopted their 12-year-old niece, Elizabeth, when her parents died. Sadly, Elizabeth herself became very ill and was told she didn't have long to live. She responded: "Oh, that is good news indeed." On her last day, she was asked how she felt. "Truly happy; if this be dying, it is a pleasant thing to die." Speaking to Mrs Newton she said: "Do not weep for me, my dear aunt, but rather rejoice and praise on my account". She was just 14 years old when she died.

How can a 14-year-old girl say she is truly happy on her death bed? We find the answer in 2 Corinthians 5 v 1-10:

> For we know that if the earthly tent we live in is destroyed, we have a building from God, an eternal house in heaven, not built by human hands. Meanwhile we groan, longing to be clothed instead with our heavenly dwelling, because when we are clothed, we will not be found naked. For while we are in this tent, we groan and are burdened, because we do not wish to be unclothed but to be clothed instead with our heavenly dwelling, so that what is mortal may be swallowed up by life. Now the one who has fashioned us for this very purpose is God, who has given us the Spirit as a deposit, guaranteeing what is to come.

Therefore we are always confident and know that as long as we are at home in the body we are away from the Lord. For we live by faith, not by sight. We are confident, I say, and would prefer to be away from the body and at home with the Lord. So we make it our goal to please him, whether we are at home in the body or away from it. For we must all appear before the judgment seat of Christ, so that each of us may receive what is due to us for the things done while in the body, whether good or bad.

The previous chapter ends by talking about the believer's body wasting away as we get older, but us being inwardly renewed as we look to what is unseen and eternal. That process of ageing brings us in chapter 5 to the reality of death. What is dying for the Christian? We're given three pictures.

1. A new house (v 1)

Dying is like moving to a new house. Verse 1 says: "For we know that if the earthly tent we live in is destroyed, we have a building from God, an eternal house in heaven, not built by human hands". The apostle Paul was a tentmaker by trade. He made ends meet by making and repairing tents, as he travelled from place to place preaching the gospel. Here he uses the tent as a picture of the body. This body, he says, is like a tent we are living in. It's our earthly home. If it is destroyed—that is, by death—Paul says we have a building from God, "an eternal house in heaven, not built by human hands". This building is not a picture of some heavenly accommodation, but rather, is referring to the resurrection body with which believers will be raised on the last day. As Romans 8 v 23 says: "We wait eagerly … for the redemption of our bodies", and Philippians 3 v 21 tells us that when the Lord Jesus Christ returns he "will transform our lowly bodies so that they will be like his glorious body". One day we will move from the tent of this body into the building of the resurrection body.

A big change such as a house-move can be unsettling, but it's also exciting. A fresh start. Especially if you're moving into something bigger and better. Paul is describing a move into a dream property, in the dream location— God's new world! It's a move from the temporary to the permanent. The tent of this body is just a temporary shelter, and after a few years the tent starts to get quite tatty and torn and doesn't keep out the wind and rain so well. But the resurrection body will be a permanent, eternal building, solid and lasting. It will never get tired or old or die. We may sometimes think that what we have now is solid and tangible, whereas the eternal future is flimsy and insubstantial. It's actually the other way round. What is solid and lasting is what we *will* have, whereas what we have now is temporary and uncertain. And one day we will trade up from the tent to the building.

In the UK, buying a house can be a nerve-wracking affair as sellers can change their minds and pull out at the last moment. All your hopes are dashed. But this deal is definitely going to go through. God has signed the contract and is waving the keys: 2 Corinthians 5 v 5 tells us he "has given us the Spirit as a deposit, guaranteeing what is to come."

Meghan Daum wrote a book called *Life would be perfect if*

I lived in that house. It tells the story of the author's endless quest for the perfect place to live, and her countless moves from one place to another. She moved to what seemed the almost perfect apartment in New York, but then wasn't satisfied once she was living there, and on it goes. Perhaps you can relate to that feeling. No house can ever satisfy our deepest longings—at least no house in this world. But it will be true of our eternal house in heaven. Life really will be perfect in our resurrection body home, and our restless longing for the perfect house now is ultimately a faint echo of our longing for that dwelling. It's not wrong to enjoy having a nice house or apartment here, but we must beware of it becoming an idol in which we invest all our hopes and dreams. It will always let us down.

2. A change of clothes (v 2-5)

The picture changes from a building to clothing in verse 2. Dying and being raised with a resurrection body will be like putting on a new and better set of clothes. Verse 4 refers to being *"clothed"*, or literally *"over-clothed"*. The idea seems to be of putting new clothes over the old ones. It's as if at the moment we're poorly dressed in these bodies which are so weak and subject to tiredness and disease and decay. We need something more substantial and lasting, and that is what the resurrection body is. When we put it on over our present outfit, then we'll be properly dressed, for ever.

For the Christian, dying, at one level, is no more traumatic than just moving house or putting on some new clothes. It's just a change, and a change for the infinitely better, though of course change can be unsettling. We become attached to what is familiar, so it's understandable if the prospect of this ultimate change feels at times unsettling. And we mustn't mishear what these pictures are telling us. The Bible doesn't trivialise death. Death remains as the last great enemy. Sometimes the actual process of dying is itself a long and painful one, and many of us know the sorrow of separation for those left behind. The Bible doesn't make light of death, but it does put it in perspective. It's not something a Christian should fear, but rather, we can face it with confidence.

And although we don't look forward to death itself, we can look forward to what lies beyond, knowing that something better, indeed the best, is yet to come. Verse 2 says: "We groan, longing to be clothed instead with our heavenly dwelling". And verse 4: "For while we are in this tent, we groan and are burdened". Sometimes when I cycle into work, it's cold and raining, and after a few minutes I realise I'm not wearing enough and I'm wet and freezing. I grit my teeth and can't wait to get into some warm, dry clothes. Life in this body can at times be like that, especially when things are tough. As Christians we groan, longing to get into the warm, dry clothes of our heavenly dwelling, the resurrection body. This isn't to say we have a death-wish. Life now is a gift from God to be lived to the full in his service, but we know the best is yet to come.

Notice, though, that Paul *doesn't want to be naked,* by which he means just existing as a spirit, apart from the body. He longs to be clothed with the resurrection body, and that is God's purpose for us; not that we should leave this body at death and live for ever as a disembodied spirit, but rather, like Jesus, we should be clothed with our glorious, transformed resurrection body.

As we saw in chapter 3, Greek philosophy at the time of the apostles taught that at death the immortal soul was released from the prison of the body. Sometimes Christians have a view of eternity which is more influenced by Greek philosophy than biblical revelation. They think that when you die, you go to heaven, as a spirit, and that is it. End of story.

But the Bible's view is that Heaven is just a station at which we stop for a while, *not the final destination.* God's eternal purpose is not that we should be unclothed, naked, disembodied, but rather clothed with resurrection bodies. That as v 4 says "what is mortal may be swallowed up by life" and put on immortality. The Spirit is our guarantee that this will happen (v 5). So every morning as you get out of bed and get dressed, you have a great daily reminder of the eternal future God has prepared you for. As you put on your clothes for the day, why not thank the Lord for the clothes you will soon be putting on—the eternal dwelling, the resurrection body.

Soul-sleep or with the Lord?

Soul-sleep is the idea that when a believer dies their soul sleeps until the final resurrection. So you as a person have no conscious existence or awareness in the period between your death and the resurrection of the body at Christ's return. It is a view which has never had wide acceptance in the church, and against which John Calvin wrote his first book in 1534.

The Bible nowhere refers to the soul sleeping, but it does refer to people dying as "falling asleep" (1 Corinthians 15 v 6; 1 Thessalonians 4 v 13,14). This is simply a picture of the wonderful reality that, for the Christian, death is only temporary, just as sleep is temporary, and raising his people from death will be as easy for God as it is for us to wake up someone who is asleep. Jesus demonstrates this with Lazarus (John 11 v 11) and the ruler's daughter who died (Matthew 9 v 24-25), both of whom Jesus said were only sleeping, before he raised them to life.

When a Christian dies, it is their body that "sleeps", awaiting the final resurrection. In fact the word cemetery comes from a Greek word meaning "a sleeping-place". A cemetery is a dormitory for the body, but in soul or spirit the believer goes immediately to be with the Lord.

For Paul, to die meant being at home with the Lord (2 Corinthians 5 v 8). Jesus assured the dying thief that "today you will be with me in paradise" (Luke 23 v 43), and his story of the rich man and Lazarus was of two men who were very much conscious after death (Luke 16 v 19-31). Moses and Elijah, though long dead, appeared at the Transfiguration talking with Jesus (Mark 9 v 4). John sees the souls of the martyrs not asleep but asking the Lord "How long?" (Revelation 6 v 9-10).

When we worship, we are joining with the spirits of believers now worshipping in heaven (Hebrews 12 v 22-24). This is why to die is "better by far" because it is to "depart and be with Christ" straight away (Philippians 1 v 23), even if the best is yet to come at the final resurrection.

3. Going home (v 6-8)

> Therefore we are always confident and know that as long as we are at home in the body we are away from the Lord. For we live by faith, not by sight. We are confident, I say, and would prefer to be away from the body and at home with the Lord.

You can't be in two places at once. If we are at home in the body (as we are now), we are away from the Lord, who is in heaven. So now we walk by faith, not sight, because we can't see him. But when we die, we will be away from this body and at home with the Lord, and that is where we would rather be. Even if for a while it means being in a disembodied state, while we wait for the resurrection body, it will be better by far because we'll be at home with the Lord. Then we won't need to live by faith any more, because we will see him and be with him, for ever.

For the Christian, to die is to go home, but home is not so much about a place as a person. It's going home *to the Lord*. Home as a concept is a place of security and love. The very idea taps into some of our deepest longings, whether it's wanting to be home for Christmas, or to make a new house into a home, or IKEA telling us that *Home is the most important place on earth*. We all long for home, and that longing is a faint echo of the longing God has planted in us for our eternal home. That is why we will never feel fully at home anywhere on this planet, because home is elsewhere. No home on earth can ultimately fulfil that longing, because our true home is with the Lord.

Here's what one Christian woman wrote when her husband died:

People die every day, but this time death was so close that I could touch it. My husband started dying long before he died. This world—our everyday rituals, the material, the future, the awareness of others—all of this very slowly crumbled around him, became dimmer, disappeared. In his eyes I could see that he had started walking towards that door. And then he went through it and left us behind. And that made me very much aware of my mortality too. But for Christians death is not the last stop. For Christians there is yet one more station. It is called "home".

Knowing this should give us confidence in the face of death. As Christians we needn't be afraid of death. Death is going home to be with the Lord for ever. But sometimes we can seem as reluctant to accept the reality of death as everyone else.

When I was a child, my grandmother spent her last months living with us as she died of cancer. I remember some well-meaning Christians coming round to pray for her healing. Here was a godly Christian woman in her seventies who was ready to go home to be with the Lord, but these dear folk just could not accept that death might be God's will for her. There is a time for seeking healing through prayer and medicine, but there is also a time for dying. Here's what someone wrote on this issue:

Some people by their obsession with physical healing seem to me to rob Christian souls of their privilege and opportunity to glorify God in the way they die. Instead of a triumphant acceptance of death, as simply one more step in the purpose of God for them, we find instead a hysterical search for healing as if it were quite impossible that it should be God's will for a Christian to die. Instead of courageous testimony, we find an attitude to death that resembles in many ways the cowardly conspiracy of silence and double-think that we find in the world. It ought not to be so.

4. Giving account (v 9-10)

But it would be wrong to think that the biblical perspective on life after death meant life before death didn't matter. Quite the opposite.

> So we make it our goal to please him, whether we are at home in the body or away from it. For we must all appear before the judgment seat of Christ, that each of us may receive what is due to us for the things done while in the body, whether good or bad. *Verses 9-10*

All of us as Christians will appear before the judgment seat of Christ, and will be called to account by him for how we have lived as his people. We will receive what is our due. We are saved by grace alone, not by works. But for the faithful, there will be some who are commended. And there will also be those described in 1 Corinthians 3 v 15 who, "will suffer loss; but yet be saved—but only as one escaping through the flames". Believers will be judged and rewarded accordingly, though not condemned, because Christ was condemned in our place. The issue is not that of eternal destiny but reward. And so 2 Corinthians 5 v 9 "We make it our goal to please him". Knowing that there is going to be this calling to account and giving of rewards is a powerful incentive for right Christian living.

There are various motivations in the Bible for living to please the Lord—there's gratitude for his grace to us; there's love for the Lord; there's living out my new identity in Christ; there's the warning that *no fruit* is a sign of *no faith*; there's the call to be like our heavenly Father; and there's this prospect of being called to account by Christ.

We should know that everything will be revealed—our secrets, our motives—and that everything we've done for him will be acknowledged and rewarded; all those things that no-one else has seen, as Jesus says in Matthew 6. Some Christians find it helpful to have an accountability group consisting of a few people with whom they meet regularly to talk about how they're doing spiritually and to pray. Knowing they'll be asked hard questions and called to give account is an incentive to continue being faithful before the next meeting. How much more so with the ultimate calling to account that we will have with the Lord Jesus!

For the Christian, dying is moving house, changing clothes, going home, and so we can face death with confidence and courage, but we also know that dying is giving account, and so we make it our aim to please the Lord.

But for the person who is not a Christian, dying is a

completely different story. To die is to appear before the judgment seat of Christ unprepared, unforgiven, and without hope. John Horsley wrote to his friend, the great British Victorian engineer, Isambard Kingdom Brunel:

I would implore you to reflect upon that hour of death which must come upon you sooner or later … Your life has been one of almost unparalleled devotion to your profession, to the exclusion, to far too great an extent, of that which was due to your God and even to your family … If you would only bring your powerful intellect to bear upon the subject which contains "the one thing needful".

As far as we know Brunel did not heed the warning. Today is as good a day as any to reflect on that hour and get ready for it. The philosopher, Cicero, said that "to study philosophy is nothing but to prepare one's self to die". God says the only way truly to prepare ourselves is to put our trust in Jesus as our Rescuer and Ruler before we meet him as our Judge.

Are there rewards in heaven?

Salvation is by grace alone, through faith alone, not through works (Ephesians 2 v 8-9). So all believers will receive the same gracious gift of salvation, regardless of how long they were Christians or how fruitful they were in serving the Lord (Matthew 20 v 10-12; 25 v 14-23).

However, although there is no condemnation for those in Christ (Romans 8 v 1), there are several passages that speak about a judgment and a calling to account by the Lord for believers (Romans 14 v 10, 12; 2 Corinthians 5 v 10). Although we are saved through faith alone, saving faith is never alone—it bears the fruit of good works, and so this judgment of believers will be according to how we have lived as believers.

The works of some who have professed faith will expose them as not having been true believers at all (Matthew 7 v 21-23). But those who are true believers will be rewarded according to their works (Matthew 10 v 41; Luke 6 v 35; 14 v 13-14; Revelation 11 v 18). But even this reward is a gracious gift by God, given that those works were a result of God's work in us (John 15 v 4-5; Philippians 2 v 12-13).

The prospect of this judgment should encourage us to keep going in good works. Our Father in heaven sees the things we do which others don't see, and he will reward us for them (Matthew 6 v 4,18). Just as there will be degrees of punishment for the unbeliever (Matthew 11 v 22; Luke 12 v 47-48; 20 v 47), so there will be degrees of reward for the believer (Luke 19 v 17, 19), though it is not clear exactly what this will look like.

Some believers will find the quality of their works exposed in this judgment, and they themselves will be saved but only as one escaping through the flames (1 Corinthians 3 v 10-15). Although no believer will be sad or regretful or envious of others and their different rewards in the age to come, it is still an encouragement to be faithful in serving the Lord now (2 Corinthians 5 v 10-11).

Chapter 5

How do we cope with bereavement?

There is nothing quite like the pain of grief when a loved one dies. The shock, the numbness, the tears, the memories, the regrets, the emptiness. It's been compared to losing a limb—in the end you adjust, but life is never the same again.

Bereavement is something Christians have to face just like everyone else. Does it make any difference being a Christian in that situation? This passage assures us that it does:

> Brothers and sisters, we do not want you to be uninformed about those who sleep in death, so that you do not grieve like the rest of mankind, who have no hope. For we believe that Jesus died and rose again, and so we believe that God will bring with Jesus those who have fallen asleep in him. According to the Lord's word, we

tell you that we who are still alive, who are left until the coming of the Lord, will certainly not precede those who have fallen asleep. For the Lord himself will come down from heaven, with a loud command, with the voice of the archangel and with the trumpet call of God, and the dead in Christ will rise first. After that, we who are still alive and are left will be caught up together with them in the clouds to meet the Lord in the air. And so we will be with the Lord for ever. There-fore encourage one another with these words.

1 Thessalonians 4 v 13-18

The Christians in the church at Thessalonica had right-ly understood that the Lord Jesus could come back any day. What they hadn't appreciated was that Christians might actually die before that happened. Now that some had died, those who had been bereaved had been knocked sideways. What had happened to their loved ones who had died? Where would they be when Christ did return? Would they miss out?

That is the issue the apostle Paul turns to address in 4 v 13, using the New Testament picture of sleep for death: "Brothers, we do not want you to be uninformed about those who sleep in death, so that you do not grieve like the rest of mankind, who have no hope." What follows was intended to comfort them, and us, in the face of bereavement within the Christian com-munity. What difference does it make being Christian when bereavement strikes?

Two things to avoid (v 13)

1. Ignorance

"Brothers and sisters, we do not want you to be uninformed about those who fall asleep" (verse 13). I don't know who it was who said *ignorance is bliss* but the Bible begs to differ. Knowledge of the truth is utterly vital.

Today there are some 23,000 licensed taxi drivers on the roads of London in their classic black cabs. They all have what is called *The Knowledge*. This is the name of what is reckoned to be the toughest taxi exam in the world, and it can take two to four years to get to the standard required to pass. The would-be cabbie has to gain a detailed knowledge of all 25,000 streets within a 6-mile radius of Charing Cross railway station.

To live rightly as a Christian in this world, you need knowledge. Not about London streets, but about what God has revealed in the Bible—and specifically here knowledge about what happens to believers who have died. It's important we know. Death may be a taboo subject in our society, but as believers we need to get to grips with death from a biblical perspective.

2. Despair

"We do not want you to ... grieve like the rest of mankind, who have no hope (verse 13). The two are connected. We avoid despair by gaining knowledge. It is this God-given knowledge that will equip us to react differently in the face of bereavement.

This isn't saying it's wrong for Christians to grieve. What *is* wrong is *grieving as those do who have no hope*.

Grief is normal and biblical. When Stephen died, we read that "Godly men buried Stephen and mourned deeply for him" (Acts 8 v 2). At the grave of his beloved friend, Lazarus, Jesus was "deeply moved in spirit and troubled", and as he wept, the Jews who were there said: "See how he loved him!" (John 11 v 33-36).

If when a loved one dies you don't feel great loss and sorrow, something is wrong. Grieving is a necessary part of the bereavement process. When people don't grieve, perhaps because they think it's inappropriate, coping with bereavement is that much harder. What Paul is against here is grieving in the way that people do *who have no hope*. He had in mind the pagan world of his day for which death spelt utter despair and total darkness. Such despair is wrong for the Christian, because we do have hope.

When my father died, my mother grieved very deeply. And although time is a healer, after 37 years of married life the loss leaves a gap which you learn to live with but which is never completely filled in this life.

But as a family we didn't grieve like those who have no hope. It was never *hopeless despair*. Part of the announcement we put in the paper read:

> *The sense of loss felt by the family is enormous, but we are greatly comforted by the knowledge that he is now at home with the Lord Jesus whom he loves and served, the same Lord Jesus who said "I am the resurrection and the life. He who believes in me will live, even though he dies".*

Grief but not despair, and knowledge is the key. It's what we know that keeps us from hopeless despair.

But what if I'm a Christian coming to terms with the death of a non-Christian loved one? In that situation do I just have to resign myself to hopeless despair?

The Bible is clear about the fate of the unbeliever, and about the fact that after death there is no second chance. But the truth is that, in the end, we just *don't know for sure* where someone stood with God. We can't read people's minds and hearts. And we are not the judge. Even someone who rejected God all through their life may have turned to him in their last moments. We just don't know for certain. Facing death does focus the mind and deathbed conversions do happen. The thief on the cross left it about as late as you possibly could before turning to the Lord. All we can do with such loved ones while they are still alive is to pray for them and be a gospel witness to them in word and deed. And when they have died, to leave them in the Lord's hands and give thanks to God for them.

Three things to believe (v 14-15)

What then is the knowledge that will keep us from despair when a Christian loved one dies? Paul highlights three things to believe.

1. Based on

"We believe that Jesus died and rose again" (verse 14). Christian hope is based on the gospel events. We believe that Jesus died and rose again. The majority of funerals I have conducted as a church minister have been for people in whom there has been little evidence of Christian faith. And yet time and again the relatives have talked of "Uncle Fred" now being in a better place. Such wishful thinking is a million miles from Christian hope, which is a sure, confident expectation of what lies ahead, based on the death and resurrection of Jesus Christ in history.

2. Brought with

"...and so we believe that God will bring with Jesus those who have fallen asleep in him" (verse 14). God will bring with Jesus at his return believers who have died. Just as God raised Jesus to life, so God will raise believers and bring them with him. For the Christian, death is not the end of the story. It's the end of a chapter. And when you turn the page, another chapter begins.

3. Better off

Far from missing out when the Lord returns, believers who have died are going to be better off than those who are alive at the time. Verse 15 tells us: "According to the Lord's word, we tell you that we who are still alive, who are left until the coming of the Lord, will certainly not precede those who have fallen asleep."

Those who are left will not "precede" them, by which Paul means they won't have any advantage over them. It seems that Christians in this church were concerned that their fellow believers who had died were in some way going to miss out when Christ returns. Far from it. Believers who have died are going to have the best seats in the house. They will accompany Jesus on his return.

Did you know that *Gandhi* was the film with the

most extras ever? 294,560 to be precise! We have a modern obsession with trivia—knowledge that is useless for anything but winning charity quiz nights or *Trivial Pursuit*. By contrast, the knowledge revealed to us in these verses is useful knowledge that gives us a sure hope in the face of bereavement. And that is why Paul wants us to have it.

Four things to happen (v 16-17)
But there's more useful information to come. There are four key events that will happen on the Last Day.

1. Return
"For the Lord himself will come down from heaven, with a loud command, with the voice of the archangel and with the trumpet call of God" (verse 16). The first thing up on the Last Day programme of events is the Lord's return. He won't just send some deputy, but rather "the Lord himself" will come down from heaven. And there'll be no missing it. It's going to be a noisy affair. Three noises are highlighted for us here, though there may well be some symbolism involved in this description.

A "loud command" is a word used of the order given by a general to his soldiers, or by a coxswain to his rowers. It is authoritative, and the reference here is probably to the Lord's command to the dead to rise from their graves. In John 5 v 28 Jesus speaks of the time "when all who are in their graves will hear his voice and come out."

There will also be the "voice of the archangel". We're pretty much in the dark about archangels. This is one of only two references in the Bible to them, the other one being in Jude v 9. So if you ever find yourself in an exam and one of the essay questions is about archangels, skip it. You'll have said everything we know in a couple of sentences.

And then there will be the "trumpet call of God". On the Last Day this trumpet blast will signal the gathering together of God's scattered people to their home. In 1 Corinthians 15 v 52 Paul says:

> The trumpet will sound, the dead will be raised imperishable, and we will be changed.

2. Resurrection

As we've seen already, Christ's return is followed by the resurrection of believers who have died: "and the dead in Christ will rise first" (verse 16). They will be the first to receive their resurrection bodies.

In the newspaper announcement about my father, we wrote that "he is now at home with the Lord", that is to say, in soul or spirit. For him, life has never been so good—it's only for those left behind that life is hard. His body, however is in the ground in a graveyard in the north of England. But when Christ returns, his body will wake as if from sleep when the Son of God gives the command. When the Bible speaks of death as sleep, as it does three times in this passage (v 13, 14, 15), it is referring to the body of the believer, which Christ will raise to life.

3. Rapture

"After that, we who are still alive and are left will be caught up together with them in the clouds" (verse 17). The word translated "caught up" means to snatch or seize forcefully. It's used in Acts 23 v 10 when Paul is being attacked by an angry mob and a military commander orders his soldiers to "take him from them by force". The equivalent Latin word is *rapere*, which is where the English word "rapture" comes from. Those believers who are still alive when the Lord returns will be raptured, "caught up together with them in the clouds".

4. Reunion

The purpose of this rapture is not to give thrills to the adrenalin junkies, but rather to bring about a reunion. "After that, we who are still alive and are left will be caught up together with them in the clouds to meet the Lord in the air. And so we will be with the Lord forever" (verse 17).

One of the most painful aspects of bereavement is being separated from those we love. I remember the last time I saw my father. My wife and I were travelling south from a holiday on a Scottish island and we stopped by at my parents' place overnight on the Saturday. The next day he made us a cooked breakfast and we went to morning church. I said goodbye at the end of the service, gave him a hug, and that was the last time I saw him. The memory of it is vivid and I treasure it.

But as a Christian I know that I'll see him again. And when we next meet, we will be reunited for ever and there will be no more goodbyes, no more separation.

Verse 17 says we who are left will be "caught up together with them", that is, with the believers who have died and who have just been raised physically. What a reunion that will be! Meeting again all our Christian loved ones who have died, together with all those believers we read about in the Bible: Abraham, Moses, Peter, Paul...

But even that is as nothing compared with the main event on the programme—**reunion with the Lord himself.** We will be "caught up together with them in the clouds to meet the Lord in the air. And so we will be with the Lord for ever". Yes, we will meet again those believers we have known and loved, but more wonderful still, we will meet the Lord and be with him for ever.

To be "in Christ" is one way the New Testament describes the Christian life (Romans 16 v 7). But the day will come when those who are in Christ will at last be with Christ. What an amazing prospect that is!

One thing to do (v 18)

It leaves us with one thing to do.

> Therefore encourage one another with these
> words.   *Verse 18*

This knowledge is revealed to us for our comfort in the face of Christian bereavement. The intention is that we use it, and use it not just to comfort ourselves but to comfort one another. True comfort in the face of bereavement comes ultimately from "these words"; that is these truths. But that isn't an excuse for giving pat responses.

Everett Koop was the US Surgeon General under Ronald Reagan. His son died when climbing in the mountains of New Hampshire, and Everett and his wife wrote about their experience.

Our family life will never be the same, but we are trusting the Lord to help us accept the empty place in our family circle and to keep us constantly aware that David is in heaven ...

In an effort to be comforting so many Christians glibly say, "God will fill the void". Instead we found that the void is really never filled, but God does make the void bearable.

If someone has just lost a Christian loved one, we must beware glib responses like *I know how you feel* or *All things work together for good*. Even reading this Bible passage to them is not an off-the-shelf, quick-fix solution. People need time and love. They need a shoulder to cry on and a listening ear. They need someone to be there for them, not just around the time of the funeral but in the difficult months ahead when the dust has settled. But the knowledge revealed in this passage is, in the end, the rock of comfort and hope on which we need to encourage one another to rebuild our lives.

Contrast this certain hope with a newspaper article written by a non-Christian about the death of his atheist father, and the burial of his ashes in their back garden. They dug a hole; they played some Mozart; they read some Shakespeare. The writer commented:

This is all death is, the end of the story.

Just The End.

It's pretty bleak, isn't it? What comfort is a piece of Mozart or Shakespeare when you've just buried your father? But if death really is the end, then there is no more comfort to be had. The question is, who is right— the Christian or the atheist?

If you were to call to a court of law each of the witnesses who saw Jesus after his resurrection, and you cross-examined them for just 15 minutes each, without a break, it would take you from breakfast on Monday until dinner on Friday to hear all of them. A total of 129 straight hours of eyewitness testimony. The resurrection of Jesus shows that Christians are not the ones doing the wishful thinking. It also shows that if we are wise, it will be our number one priority to make sure we get right with God before the day of the Lord comes.

Will we recognise loved ones?

We will certainly recognise one another in the coming kingdom. The prospect of reunion with loved ones in 1 Thessalonians 4 v 11-18 would be of little comfort if this were not the case. The resurrection body with which we will be raised is this present body, not an unrelated brand new one, but gloriously transformed.

This principle of both continuity and transformation is illustrated in 1 Corinthians 15 v 37-38 by a seed and the plant which grows from it. The disciples recognised

Jesus in his resurrection body as the same Jesus they had known before, although presumably raised in his prime and perfection, which may account for why, on occasion, they didn't immediately recognise him (Luke 24 v 16).

It seems we will even recognise one another in heaven before our bodies are raised, as Moses and Elijah were recognised by the disciples at the Transfiguration (Luke 9 v 33); and in the story Jesus told in Luke 16 v 19-31 the rich man recognised the poor man, Lazarus, who used to beg at his gates.

And there will be not just recognition but transformed relationship. We will enjoy fellowship with one another as well as with Christ, as we take our places at the feast with Abraham, Isaac and Jacob (Matthew 8 v 11). But our relationships will also be transformed. Jesus hinted at this in Matthew 12 v 48-50, saying that those who did his Father's will were now his brother, sister and mother, rather than just those in his blood family. And if married now, although we will still know our believing spouses then, we will no longer be married to them, as there will be no marriage in heaven (Luke 20 v 34-36). Instead we will enjoy the reality which marriage pictures, the union of Christ with his people.

And presumably all our relationships then will be as deep as that enjoyed in the best marriage now. And if we are aware of loved ones absent because they didn't believe, somehow we won't be sad and miss them, for in the age to come tears and sorrow will be a thing of the past (Revelation 21 v 4).

Is eternal judgment fair?

We have a curious relationship with judgment. We instinctively react against people judging us, but we all know that wrongdoing deserves punishment. So it's a good thing that God is perfectly just: the universe would be a terrible place if he wasn't. But we may feel that eternal judgment is disproportionate as a punishment for 70 years of rejecting God. Here are four things to consider.

First, from our perspective now, we're going to struggle to see what is truly right, because we don't see clearly how utterly holy God is and how sinful we are. But we need to trust him that he will do what is right. The Bible repeatedly assures us that God's judgment will be utterly right and fair (Psalm 9 v 8).

Second, the punishment that fits a crime doesn't relate to how long it took to commit the crime. How long does it take to murder someone? It takes just a second to shoot someone. But most people agree that life imprisonment, at the very least, is a fitting punishment for that crime.

Third, the seriousness of a crime depends on who you commit it against. If you cut a worm in half, that's not so bad. Do it to your neighbour's dog and it's more serious. To a child, even more so. To the President or Queen, it's more serious still. So what if our crime is against God, the owner and ruler of the universe?

And **fourth**, the reason that hell is ongoing and eternal may be that rebels *continue* in rebellion against God in eternity, because there is no repentance in hell.

Chapter 6

What will life be like in eternity?

rthur Stace was born in the slums of Sydney to alcoholic parents. He was brought up in poverty, became a heavy drinker and ended up on the streets, but then one night in 1930 he heard the good news about Jesus and began to follow him.

Two years later he heard a sermon about eternity in which the preacher said:

> *"Eternity, eternity, I wish that I could sound or shout that word to everyone in the streets of Sydney. You've got to meet it; where will you spend eternity?"*

The impression it made set the course of Arthur's life. Several mornings a week, for the next 35 years, he went around the streets of Sydney and wrote in chalk the word *Eternity* on pavements, walls, anywhere he could think of. Workers arriving in the city in the morning would see the word freshly written everywhere, but for over 20 years no-one knew who was doing it. "The man who writes eternity" became a legend in Sydney.

Where will you spend eternity?

It's not something people think about much, if at all, in the day-to-day of their busy lives, and yet what could be more important?

When people speak of the "afterlife", it gives the impression that the life we have now is the main event and what comes after is just some tag-on. Maths isn't my strong-point, but even I can work out that if *now* is 70 or 80 years and *what comes after* lasts for ever, *now* cannot be the main event. The eternal future is not the afterlife. Instead our experience now might be described as the pre-life. The main event is still to come.

Jesus laid before people the stark alternatives of "eternal punishment" and "eternal life" (Matthew 25 v 46). It's an issue which the last book of the Bible will not let us forget. Revelation 20 ends with a vision of the defeat of God's enemies and the final judgment. Then in the last two chapters of the book the focus turns to the eternal future that God has prepared for his people. But what is the point of God revealing this to us? Why not just get on with the here-and-now? As far as God is concerned, this vision of the future is the answer—but what was the question?

The very last verse reminds us that the book of Revelation is actually a letter. 22 v 21: "The grace of the Lord Jesus be with God's people" is a standard ending in New Testament letters. This is a letter which, like the rest of the letters in the New Testament, was written to help Christians facing particular problems. Chapters 2 – 3 reveal at least four—**opposition** (some of the Christians were having a tough time from others because of their faith); **compromise** (some were going astray in their beliefs and behaviour); **half-heartedness** (some were lukewarm in their commitment); and **cold-heartedness** (some were not being loving).

How do you encourage Christians to keep going in those circumstances? That is the question. The answer is this vision of the eternal future. If you can relate to any of those first-century struggles, this vision of the future is what you need. It's given in the first place to encourage those who profess Christian faith to keep going. But if you're not a Christian this issue of where you will spend eternity is more important than anything else you've been thinking about so far this week.

God's new world

Place

What God has in store for his people in eternity is life in a new world which is not just spiritual but physical. A new heaven and earth.

> Then I saw a new heaven and a new earth, for the first heaven and the first earth had passed away.
> *Revelation 21 v 1*

This present creation will be completely renewed, as God proclaims in v 5: "I am making everything new!". That doesn't mean God will scrap this creation and start again from scratch, creating everything again out of nothing. The new universe will be this present one radically transformed and renewed, just as our bodies will be.

If we're Christian, in the end we're not going to go to heaven. God has got much bigger plans for us than that! If I die tomorrow, I will go to heaven, but that is just a stop on the journey, not the final destination. Like touching down at Singapore on my way to Australia. The destination is the new universe that God will raise from the ashes of this one. And what a place it will be.

It's so hard to imagine that John has to resort to telling us what is *not* there: "There was no longer any sea" (verse 1). That doesn't mean there's no sailing in God's new world! Sea in the Bible is often used as a symbol for uncontrollable forces that threaten God's people. All the threats of the old world will be gone. But there's more:

> He will wipe every tear from their eyes. There will be no more death or mourning or crying or pain, for the old order of things has passed away.
>
> *Verse 4*

Imagine that! No tears, because there's nothing to be sad about any more. No loss, disappointment, heartache, stress, tragedy or boredom. And no death. No more funerals, no more separation, no more getting ill and old.

Verse 2 goes on: "I saw the Holy City; the new Jerusalem, coming down out of heaven from God". In chapter 21, John is taken on a guided tour of this new city. On one level the city seems to be just another way of picturing this new world where God's people will live. It's the same idea as the new heaven and earth but using a different picture.

And notice in v 2 and 10 that rather than us going to heaven, *the new world comes down to us*. John is shown round the wall and the gates and the foundations. We need to bear in mind that this is a vision. We're not saying that if a video camera could beam back images from the future, this is what would appear on your screen. God is revealing future reality symbolically.

We learn that **it's a place of security**, symbolised in v 12 by "a great high wall", and in v 25 by the detail that "On no day will its gates ever be shut, for there will be no night there". No threats or danger any more. Total safety and security. Imagine living in a world in which you never needed to lock your house or your car!

As chapter 22 begins, the tour reaches the city centre:

> Then the angel showed me the river of the water of life, as clear as crystal, flowing from the throne of God and of the Lamb down the middle of the great street of the city. On each side of the river stood the tree of life. *22 v 1*

It reminds us of where the whole human drama began, back in the Garden of Eden in Genesis 2. A river flowed out of Eden and in the middle of the garden was the tree of life, but because of their disobedience, the first people were thrown out. The whole Bible story is about how God has made for us a way back to that tree and to life without the curse of Genesis 3 hanging over it like a dark cloud. In the new creation: "No longer will there be any curse" (22 v 3).

In all of us there is a deep-rooted longing for life in this sort of place, because, as Ecclesiastes 3 v 11 says, God has "set eternity in the human heart". Without knowing it, maybe that is why we long for summer holidays in dream locations, because we have a sense that we were created for such places. When life is hard, perhaps what keeps you going is thinking of the next holiday you have planned. As Christians we need to be thinking often about the new world if we're to keep going in the faith. When did you last think beyond your next holiday to eternity?

Relationship

However, you could be in the most beautiful place but be miserable because relationships have gone wrong or you're lonely. Life is about relationship, not just location.

The Bible story begins in a garden but ends in a city, because what lies ahead is life in community as the people of God, where we will enjoy perfect relationships with one another. But more than this, at the heart of God's new world will be relationship with God himself:

> And I heard a loud voice from the throne saying, "Look! God's dwelling-place is now among the people, and he will dwell with them. They will be his people, and God himself will be with them and be their God."
>
> *Revelation 21 v 3*

This is the ultimate blessing which the whole Bible story is heading towards. This is what we were created for. The key thing about the new city is that **God is there**—in 21 v 22 the Lord is the temple, and in v 23 his glory floods the city with light.

Notice how intimate the relationship is: "He will wipe every tear from their eyes" (v 4). A picture, but one of great intimacy and loving care. And in v 7 God says: "I will be their God and they will be my children". In 22 v 4 it says of his people that "They will see his face". That is closeness, not relationship at a distance. And it gives the strange detail that "his name will be on their foreheads". In the Old Testament, God's name was on the forehead of the high priest, but now all of God's people will enjoy intimate fellowship with God, serving him as priests, and (v 5) reigning with him as kings.

God has made us for relationship with himself. The breakdown of that relationship is the source of all our sorrows. Its restoration will be the source of every blessing. This is what lies ahead for God's people who keep going in faith, in the face of all the struggles and temptations.

Warning

21 v 7 says: "Those who are victorious will inherit all this, and I will be their God and they will be my children". The promise is an encouragement but also a warning, which is spelled out in the next verses:

> But the cowardly, the unbelieving, the vile, the murderers, the sexually immoral, those who prac-

tise magic arts, the idolaters and all liars—they
will be consigned to the fiery lake of burning
sulphur. This is the second death. *21 v 8-9*

The list isn't random. It picks up on sins that were
plaguing the first-century churches of chapters 2 – 3. So
in 2 v 10 God urges those in Smyrna not to fear opposition—the cowardly are those who will refuse to take
a stand for Christ and so prove faithless. Sexual immo-
rality and idolatry were infecting the churches through
false teaching. And "liars" refers to those who claim to
be Christian but whose lives or beliefs deny it.

Eternity, eternity, where will you spend eternity? Faced
with these contrasting eternal futures, our instinctive
response may be: "I need to warn my loved ones, my
friends and colleagues and neighbours". That is a right
and loving response, but in the first place the message
of this letter is to encourage those who *already profess
faith* to keep going, and to warn them about the con-
sequences of compromising and giving up. This eternal
perspective is what Christians need if they are to over-
come and conquer. If we just keep our heads down and
think about today and tomorrow, the engine won't be
getting the fuel it needs to keep going. The car of faith
runs on the fuel of eternity.

God's new people

But eternity is not just about God's new world but also
God's new people. Part of the motivation to keep going
is seeing what we will one day become.

I imagine the average caterpillar must have times

when it feels like giving up—crawling around on a leaf all day, at the mercy of every bird that happens to fly by. But then it sees a stunningly beautiful butterfly flutter past with its multi-coloured wings, enjoying the freedom of the open skies, and the caterpillar thinks to itself: *It is worth it. That is what I'm going to be like one day. I'd forgotten where I'm heading. I'm on a journey from egg to caterpillar to chrysalis to butterfly.* And so with ourselves; it's easy to get discouraged and disillusioned when we look at the state of our own lives or those around us who profess faith. It's easy to feel: *"What's the point? Let's face it, we're just caterpillars, nothing more."* But in chapter 21 God reveals what his people will one day become. He uses two pictures.

The glorious bride

In 17 v 1 an angel says to John: "Come, I will show you the punishment of the great prostitute". The prostitute is a picture of the world in all its ugly rejection of God. But now in 21 v 9 an angel says to John: "Come, I will show you the bride, the wife of the Lamb", described in v 2 as "a bride beautifully dressed for her husband". What a contrast. And what a contrast to the churches of chapters 2 – 3 with all their problems and imperfections. It's like one of those detergent adverts with the kid covered in mud and then the same football shirt spotlessly white. On that day we will be not just forgiven through Christ but also completely free from sin. That prospect is a motivation to godly living now. Live in line with the person you one day will be.

The glorious city

The second picture of what God's people will be like is the glorious city. In 21 v 2 John says:

> I saw the Holy City, the new Jerusalem, coming down out of heaven from God, prepared as a bride beautifully dressed for her husband.

The bride and the city are pictures of the same thing— *God's new people as they will be.* We saw before that the city represents the place where God's people will live, but now we see that it also represents the people themselves. The picture works on both levels. It may seem a bit odd to picture people as a city, but elsewhere in the Bible God's people are pictured as a temple which God is building, so it's just a development of that.

Once we see this, it makes sense of some of the details. In v 15-17 we have detailed measurements of the city. It's a perfect cube with each side measuring 12,000 stadia (over 2,000 km or 1,300 miles). In v 17 the wall is 144 cubits thick. The figures echo the numbers in chapter 7 which symbolised the full number of God's people. These measurements speak of security; the full number of God's true people will be there. It's the same point in v 18-21 with the foundations made of different kinds of precious stones. These 12 stones were on the breastplate which the high priest wore in the Old Testament, and represented the 12 tribes of Israel. These precious stones represent all God's people. And the materials the city is made of symbolise how God's people will reflect his glory—v 11: "It shone with the glory of God, and its brilliance was like that of a very precious jewel".

When you go past a construction site, there is sometimes a big board with a computer-generated image of what the building will be like when it's finished. But for now, all you see on the site is dirt and bricks and holes in the ground. It looks like complete chaos. But that picture lifts your eyes to what the finished construction will be like, and is a motivation no doubt for the builders just as much as for prospective buyers. In this vision God gives us his picture of what his people will one day be like. When we look at our own lives and the state of the church, we may be tempted to despair, but the picture of the finished construction is given to encourage us to keep going in faithfulness and godliness, living transformed lives which reflect what we will be like in the age to come.

God's final appeal
Future certainties

But some would say this vision is just wishful thinking, whistling in the dark—pure escapism which the apostle John needed to get himself through his time of exile on the island of Patmos. In 22 v 6 Jesus reminds us, through his angel, that "these words are trustworthy and true". This isn't just a dream the apostle John had or wishful thinking. It's a revelation from God. We have Jesus' word on it, the Jesus who died and was raised to life and is coming soon. In v 7 Jesus assures us: "Behold, I am coming soon!" It is his coming that will bring all this about.

But it's now 2,000 years since Jesus said he was coming soon! "Soon" could mean that when he does come it will be sudden; or it could mean there is now no other event in God's plan that needs to happen before this final one; or it could be just viewing time from the perspective of God, for whom a day is like a thousand years.

But come he surely will. He is (v 13) the "Alpha and Omega, the First and the Last, the Beginning and the End". Everything is in his sovereign control, so nothing can stop him. As God's people we should long for and pray for that day:

> The Spirit and the bride say "Come!" …"Yes, I am coming soon." Amen. Come Lord Jesus.
>
> *Verses 17, 20*

Present choices

But these future certainties leave us with present choices. In these final verses there are repeated promises of blessing for those who keep the words of the prophecy (v 7), but also warnings for those who don't (v 18-19).

Eternity, eternity, where will you spend eternity?

God is making his final appeal—an appeal in v 17 to "take the free gift of the water of life". It's an invitation to those who have not yet found forgiveness through Jesus, but also, and in the first place, an appeal to the Christian to keep going in faithfulness to Christ as we face the struggles, temptations and pressures of life in this world. In the end it is the one who conquers who will inherit all this.

What is the soul or spirit?

A person is made up of a material body and a non-material "inner person"—a soul or spirit. This inner person is often referred to as the soul or spirit. Some take these to be two separate parts, as 1 Thessalonians 5 v 23 might seem to imply. But this could just be a way of saying "the whole person". The Bible does seem to use these two different words for what is essentially the same thing. So in Luke 1 v 46-47 Mary says: "My soul glorifies the Lord and my spirit rejoices in God my Saviour".

We relate to God as a whole person—1 Cor 7 v 34 talks about being "devoted to the Lord in both body and spirit" and in 2 Cor 7 v 1 we are told "Let us purify ourselves from everything that contaminates body and spirit".

At death the spirit or soul is separated from the body. Ecclesiastes 12 v 7: "the dust returns to the ground it came from, and the spirit returns to God who gave it". Just before Jesus died he cried out: "Father, into your hands I commit my spirit". The soul cannot die. Jesus said, "Do not be afraid of those who kill the body but cannot kill the soul" (Matthew 10 v 28). The soul lives on for ever, and that is why we must do everything we can to make sure our souls are saved.

Jesus asked: "What good is it for someone to gain the whole world, yet forfeit their soul?" (Mark 8 v 36). At death the soul of the believer goes immediately to be with the Lord and that of the unbeliever to a place of separation from him (Luke 16 v 19-31). At the return of Christ, the dead will all be raised physically, and body and soul will be reunited. Then after the final judgment, unbelievers "will go away to eternal punishment, but the righteous to eternal life" (Matthew 25 v 46).

Will we see our pets again?

Pets bring companionship and happiness into the lives of so many, and when they die it can be a huge sadness. Animals are a wonderful part of the world God has made and they clearly matter to him. After the Flood the covenant which God established never to flood the earth again was not just with Noah but with every living creature (Genesis 9 v 9-10). The earth is full of God's creatures and he lovingly cares for them (Psalm 104 v 24-30). He feeds the birds (Matthew 6 v 26) and not even a sparrow is forgotten by him (Luke 12 v 6), and he expects us to reflect his care in our treatment of animals (Proverbs 12 v 10).

Just as animals are part of God's good creation now, so there is good reason to believe they will be part of the age to come. God's ultimate purpose is the renewal of all things (Matthew 19 v 28), with this present creation one day being renewed and restored – and that does seem to include animals. "The wolf shall dwell with the lamb, and the leopard shall lie down with the young goat" (Isaiah 11 v 6-9). The whole of creation looks forward to that day when it will be set free from its bondage to decay (Romans 8 v 21)—the day when "every creature in heaven and on earth and under the earth and on the sea" will be praising God (Revelation 5 v 13).

The biblical vision of the future is of God's people and the creation being renewed and redeemed, not of God starting again and creating out of nothing. Does that mean he will raise some or all animals to life? The Bible simply doesn't give a definitive answer. But what is clear is that we will only be there to enjoy eternity with them if we trust in Christ. It would be tragic if our beloved pets made it to God's new world but we ourselves didn't!

Conclusion

Fast-forward in your mind to that time when you yourself are facing death. Perhaps you will be an older person knowing that the end of your life on earth is approaching; or perhaps you will be a younger person who has just been told by a doctor that you do not have long to live.

Whatever the case, you are now standing at the door of death and know that you will soon have to go through it. Where will you turn in the Bible? What passage will sustain and comfort you? Perhaps by that stage concentration is hard and you are not able to take much in. You need a few simple truths to hold on to. What better verses to meditate on than those of Psalm 23, the best-known and best-loved of all the psalms, and one which is ideally suited for such a time as this. This psalm would be a good one to learn by heart, so that it is there in our minds to strengthen our faith when that day comes. David pictures the Lord as both his shepherd and his host, caring for him.

The LORD as my shepherd (v 1-4)

The LORD is my shepherd, I lack nothing.
He makes me lie down in green pastures,
    he leads me beside quiet waters,
    he refreshes my soul.
He guides me along the right paths
    for his name's sake.
Even though I walk through the darkest valley,
I will fear no evil, for you are with me;
your rod and your staff, they comfort me.

David had himself been a shepherd and so knew all about what it meant to look after the flock. Here he pictures the Lord personally caring for him as "my shepherd." As shepherd, the Lord provides for all our needs, so that "I lack nothing" (v 1). He spiritually feeds, refreshes and restores us, and shows us the right way to live (v 2). Even though David knew that dark days lay ahead, he didn't give way to fear because he knew that the Lord was with him, and would give him all the spiritual protection he needed, just as David himself used to protect the sheep from attack with his rod and staff (v 4).

One of the scary things about dying is that no-one can walk into that darkest valley with us. We have to go it alone. Friends and family may walk with us through life, but as we enter the valley of the shadow of death, we have to let go of their hand, say goodbye and walk on alone. But with the Lord at our side we have nothing to fear. He will stick by us as we head off down that dark path. No-one else can do this for us—no other teacher or philosopher or leader.

If David found this a comfort, how much more should we, now that this shepherd has entered our world in the person of God's Son. Jesus said:

> "I am the good shepherd. The good shepherd lays
> down his life for the sheep."   *John 10 v 11*

The good Shepherd died for our sins and then took up his life again, is alive today and promises never to leave us or forsake us if we trust in him. Knowing this we can say with David as we face death: "I fear no evil."

Another David—David Watson—was a well-known and influential English Christian leader, who died in 1984 at the age of 51. He wrote a personal account of his battle with cancer in a book called *Fear no evil*. It is a fitting title. Once we put our trust in the Lord, we have nothing to fear. He will stay with us through good times and bad—in green pastures and by still waters, but also through the darkest valleys, and in the end through the darkest of them all, through death itself, and out into the sunshine of his eternal kingdom on the other side.

The Lord as my host (v 5-6)

> You prepare a table before me
>   in the presence of my enemies.
> You anoint my head with oil; my cup overflows.

> Surely your goodness and love will follow me
> > all the days of my life,
> and I will dwell in the house of the LORD for ever.

In the second half of the psalm we move indoors, as the picture changes from that of a sheep in a flock to a guest at a banquet. The Lord is the ultimate Host, providing for us generously and abundantly. He prepares the table, anoints our head with oil and fills our cup to overflowing. Although David's enemies had not gone away (v 5), and we too know that our struggle with "spiritual forces of evil" will continue to the end (Ephesians 6 v 12), we can take heart with David that the Lord will keep providing for our every need, "all the days of my life", and his goodness and love will pursue us and never give up.

But wonderfully, his provision is not just for this life but also for the life to come—"I will dwell in the house of the Lord for ever" (v 6). If we trust in Jesus, when we die we will be welcomed into the Father's house of which Jesus spoke (John 14 v 2), and there we will take our place at the ultimate banquet, the wedding supper of the Lamb (Revelation 19 v 9). And so we will be with the Lord for ever.

It's easy to speak of death with bravado when it's a long way off; it's less easy when it's staring you in the face. But if we're those who, like David, know the Lord personally as our shepherd and host, we have nothing to fear. We can face death with courage and conviction and peace, because we know the one "who has destroyed death and has brought life and immortality to light through the gospel" (2 Timothy 1 v 10).

How can we talk to others about God's judgment?

The devil's lie in the Garden of Eden was that God won't judge (Genesis 3 v 4). It's a lie that our culture has swallowed unthinkingly. The modern mantra is that we must just accept everyone as they are and not judge. And so, we reckon, if *we* shouldn't judge, God shouldn't either.

But although our culture is allergic to judgment, what it *does* believe in is *justice*, and we can appeal to this instinct as a way into talking about eternal judgment. People long for justice. When a sexual abuser is arrested and convicted, we nod with grim satisfaction. When a dictator is toppled, people dance in the streets. When a war criminal is called to account for acts of genocide, people cheer. But when an oppressor dies without facing justice, we groan with sadness that they have "got away with it".

This is why we should welcome the idea of God's final judgment. We can honestly say that *no one* will get away with *anything*. God will judge justly with complete and detailed knowledge of every motivation and thought. Nothing will be left out. All wrongs will be righted. Justice is what we want. Justice is what is coming. Judgment is actually good news.

thegoodbook
COMPANY

BIBLICAL | RELEVANT | ACCESSIBLE

At The Good Book Company, we are dedicated to helping Christians and local churches grow. We believe that God's growth process always starts with hearing clearly what he has said to us through his timeless word—the Bible.

Ever since we opened our doors in 1991, we have been striving to produce resources that honour God in the way the Bible is used. We have grown to become an international provider of user-friendly resources to the Christian community, with believers of all backgrounds and denominations using our Bible studies, books, evangelistic resources, DVD-based courses and training events.

We want to equip ordinary Christians to live for Christ day by day, and churches to grow in their knowledge of God, their love for one another, and the effectiveness of their outreach.

Call us for a discussion of your needs or visit one of our local websites for more information on the resources and services we provide.

Your friends at The Good Book Company

UK & EUROPE		thegoodbook.co.uk	0333 123 0880
NORTH AMERICA		thegoodbook.com	866 244 2165
AUSTRALIA		thegoodbook.com.au	(02) 9564 3555
NEW ZEALAND		thegoodbook.co.nz	(+64) 3 343 2463

 WWW.CHRISTIANITYEXPLORED.ORG
Our partner site is a great place for those exploring the Christian faith, with a clear explanation of the good news, powerful testimonies and answers to difficult questions.